The Sex Education Book For Boys 8-12 year olds

Everything boys need to know about Sex, Puberty, Relationship, Boundaries and Growing Up

Elizabeth A. Kille

TABLE OF CONTENT

Introduction

Puberty can seem like a big, scary word, but don't worry - we're all in this together.

As a mom who's been through it with my son, I remember how confusing and overwhelming those changes can feel.

But trust me, it's all part of an incredible journey that every single one of us goes through.

So, what exactly is puberty? It's kind of like your body's way of leveling up from being a kid to becoming a teenager.

It's when your brain starts sending out special hormones that kick-start a whole bunch of physical and emotional changes.

And let me tell you, these changes can be pretty wild.

One day, you might notice that you're suddenly shooting up like a beanstalk, leaving those old clothes in the dust.

Or maybe your voice starts cracking and dropping, making you sound like a different person.

You might even start sprouting hair in places you've never had it before (hello, armpits and facial fuzz!).

But puberty isn't just about the external stuff. It's also a time when your emotions can feel like a rollercoaster, with mood swings and new feelings you've never experienced before.

One minute you're on top of the world, and the next, you're feeling down in the dumps for no apparent reason.

Now, I know all of this might sound a bit daunting, but here's the thing: puberty is an incredible, mind-blowing process that every single person goes through.

It's your body's way of transforming you from a kid into a young adult, complete with all the cool new abilities and superpowers that come with it.

And trust me, as weird and awkward as it might seem at times, you're not alone in this journey.

All your friends, classmates, and millions of other kids around the world are going through the same thing.

It's like you're all part of this secret club, where you get to experience all the crazy changes together.

So, why does puberty even matter? Well, aside from turning you into a full-fledged teenager, it's also a time when you start discovering who you are.

You might develop new interests, hobbies, and passions that will shape the person you'll become.

It's a chance to explore your identity, figure out what's important to you, and start making decisions that will impact your future.

And let's not forget, puberty is also the gateway to some pretty cool stuff.

Once you've gone through it, you'll be able to do things like grow taller, build muscle, and even have kids of your own someday (but let's not get ahead of ourselves here!).

Look, I know puberty can be a wild ride, but it's also an amazing, once-in-a-lifetime experience that you'll never forget.

So, buckle up, boys, and get ready for the adventure of a lifetime. We're all in this together, and with a little guidance and a whole lot of laughter, we'll make it through to the other side, stronger, wiser, and awesome.

Chapter One

Understanding Puberty

By now, you know puberty is all about those crazy changes your body goes through as you transition from a kid to a full-blown teenager. But what exactly is happening under the hood?

Well, buckle up, because it's about to get wild!

You see, there's this thing called hormones. Think of them as tiny chemical messengers that travel through your body, telling it what to do and when to do it. And during puberty, your brain starts pumping out a whole bunch of new hormones, like testosterone for us guys.

These hormones are like the superheroes of your body, with the power to make some seriously epic transformations happen. And trust me, you're going to notice the effects!

One of the biggest changes is the growth spurt. Suddenly, you might feel like you're outgrowing your clothes faster than you can buy new ones. That's because those hormones are telling your bones to start growing like crazy, making you taller and bigger in ways you never imagined.

And then there's the voice change. You know how sometimes your voice cracks and goes all over the place, making you sound like you're caught between a deep baritone and a squeaky mouse? That's because those pesky hormones are also affecting your vocal cords, making them thicker and longer, giving you that manly tone you've always dreamed of (even if it takes a little practice to control).

But wait, there's more! Hormones also trigger the growth of body hair in places you've never had it before. Yep, I'm talking about those fuzzy friends that start sprouting up under your arms, on your legs, and even on your face (hello, mustache!). It might seem a bit weird at first, but it's all part of becoming a man.

And let's not forget about acne. Those darn hormones can also cause an increase in oil production, which can lead to clogged pores and those pesky pimples that seem to pop up at the worst possible times. Don't worry, though, with a good skincare routine and a little patience, you'll get through it like a champ.

Now, I know all these physical changes can be a lot to handle, but there's another side to puberty that's just as important: the emotional rollercoaster.

You see, those hormones don't just affect your body; they also have a major impact on your mood and emotions. One minute you might feel on top of the world, and the next, you're feeling angry, frustrated, or even a little down in the dumps.

It's normal to experience mood swings, anxiety, and even some occasional moodiness during this time. Your emotions are like a wild bucking bronco, and you're just trying to hold on for dear life!

But here's the thing, guys: all of these changes, as crazy as they might seem, are completely natural and normal. They're your body's way of preparing you for the next stage of life, transforming you from a kid into a young adult with all the exciting experiences and responsibilities that come with it.

So, embrace the chaos! Laugh at the awkward moments, be patient with yourself, and know that you're not alone in this journey. Every single one of your friends is going through the same thing, and together, you'll make it through to the other side, stronger, more confident, and awesome.

Remember, puberty is an incredible adventure, and you're the star of the show. So, buckle up, hold on tight, and get ready for the ride of your life.

Physical Changes (growth spurts, voice changes, facial hair)

Get ready, because your body is about to level up in some seriously cool (and maybe a little bit weird) ways!

First up, the growth spurt. You know how you used to be one of the shortest kids in your class? Well, say goodbye to those days, because puberty is going to make you shoot up like a rocket! One day, you'll wake up and suddenly realize that you're towering over your friends, your pants are too short, and you can finally reach that top shelf in the kitchen (score!).

This growth spurt is all thanks to those hormones we talked about earlier. They're like a secret signal telling your bones to start growing at an insane pace. And we're not just talking about getting taller, either. Your hands, feet, and even your nose might start growing, too! It's like your body is transforming into a whole new, bigger, and better version of itself.

Now, as awesome as it is to finally be the tallest one in the room, this growth spurt can also come with some growing pains. You might experience achy joints, sore muscles, and even a few awkward stumbles as you adjust to your new size. But don't worry, it's all part of the process, and it'll be worth it when you're towering over everyone else!

Next up, the voice changes. Remember when we talked about how those hormones can make your vocal cords thicker and longer?

Well, get ready for your voice to start cracking and dropping like crazy! One minute, you might sound like your normal self, and the next, you're practically growling like a bear.

This voice change can be both hilarious and a little embarrassing at times. You might find yourself suddenly struggling to hit those high notes in your favorite songs or accidentally scaring your little sister with your newfound baritone. But trust me, it's all part of the journey to developing that deep, manly voice you've always wanted.

And speaking of manly, let's talk about facial hair. Yep, you read that right – those same hormones that are making you taller and changing your voice are also responsible for the fuzz that starts sprouting up on your face, your chest, and even your legs!

At first, it might just be a few stray hairs here and there, but before you know it, you'll be rocking a full-blown mustache or beard (if you're lucky enough to inherit those genes, that is). And while it might seem a little weird at first, having facial hair is a surefire sign that you're well on your way to becoming a full-fledged man.

Of course, with great facial hair comes great responsibility. You'll need to learn how to groom and maintain it properly, which means investing in a good razor, shaving cream, and maybe even a little bit of patience (no one wants a patchy beard!).

But hey, at least you'll finally be able to join the ranks of your dad, uncles, and all the other dudes in your life who rock that rugged, manly look.

Now, I know all these changes can seem a bit overwhelming at times, but trust me, they're all part of the incredible journey that is puberty. Sure, you might feel a little awkward or self-conscious as your body transforms, but remember, every single one of your friends is going through the same thing.

So, embrace the chaos! Laugh at the cracking voices and unexpected hair growth. And most importantly, be patient with yourself. Puberty is a process, and it takes time to adjust to all these new changes.

Before you know it, you'll be rocking your new height, your deep voice, and maybe even a killer mustache (if you're lucky!). And when you look back on this time, you'll realize that it was all part of the incredible adventure that helped shape you into the awesome young man you've become.

Hormonal Changes

Hormones are like tiny chemical messengers that travel through your bloodstream, telling your body what to do and when to do it. And during puberty, your brain starts pumping out a whole new crew of hormones that take over the control room.

For us fellas, the star of the show is a hormone called testosterone. This bad boy is responsible for a lot of the physical changes we go through, like deeper voices, facial hair growth, and even those random, awkward boners that pop up out of nowhere (don't worry, we've all been there!).

Testosterone is like the ringleader of the puberty circus, telling your body to start bulking up with more muscle, getting taller, and pretty much transforming you from a scrawny kid into a full-blown man. It's kind of like your own personal superhero serum, just without the spandex costume (although that could be kind of cool, too!).

But testosterone isn't the only hormone getting in on the action. There's also a whole squad of other hormones, like growth hormone, that help fuel that epic growth spurt we talked about earlier. These guys work together like a well-oiled machine, making sure your body is changing and developing at just the right pace.

Now, as awesome as all these hormonal changes are, they can also have some pretty wild side effects. You might find yourself feeling more emotional than usual, with mood swings that make you want to laugh one minute and cry the next. Or maybe you'll start getting randomly angry or frustrated over the smallest things (sorry, Mom and Dad!).

That's because these hormones don't just affect your physical body – they also have a major impact on your brain and emotions. It's like they're turning up the volume on every feeling you've ever had, making even the most trivial things seem like a huge deal.

But don't worry, guys, these emotional rollercoasters are totally normal and just part of the puberty package. Trust me, we've all been there, riding the waves of hormonal changes and trying our best to keep it together.

The important thing is to be patient with yourselves and remember that it's all just a phase. These hormone-fueled mood swings and emotional outbursts will eventually level out as your body gets used to all the new changes.

In the meantime, try to find healthy ways to cope with all those big feelings. Talk to your friends, your parents, or a trusted adult about what you're going through. Exercise is also a great way to blow off some steam and release any pent-up energy or frustration.

And above all, don't be too hard on yourselves. Puberty is a wild ride, and it's normal to feel a little out of control sometimes. Just remember that you're not alone in this journey and that every single one of your friends is going through the same hormonal chaos.

So, embrace the craziness, laugh at the awkward moments, and know that with time and patience, you'll eventually find your groove and learn to navigate these hormone-fueled waters like a pro. After all, you're becoming a man – and that's something to be truly proud of.

Emotions and Mood Swings

One minute you're feeling on top of the world like you could conquer anything. The next, you're moody, irritable, and ready to snap at the slightest thing. Sound familiar? Welcome to the emotional rollercoaster that is puberty!

As your body goes through all these crazy physical changes, your emotions are along for the ride too. Those same hormones that are making you taller and hairier are also messing with your brain chemistry, turning your feelings into a wild bucking bronco that's nearly impossible to stay on top of.

Intense mood swings are normal during this time. One second you might be laughing hysterically with your friends, and the next, you're fighting back tears over something that wouldn't have even fazed you a few months ago. It's like someone flipped an emotional switch, and you can't control the ups and downs.

And let's not forget about the anger and frustration that can come out of nowhere. Suddenly, the smallest things – your sister borrowing your favorite shirt, your mom asking you to take out the trash – can feel like the biggest deal in the world, making you want to lash out or retreat to your room and sulk.

It's all part of the puberty package, guys. As your hormones surge and your brain continues developing, you might find yourself feeling angrier, sadder, or just plain moodier than usual. And that's okay! It doesn't mean there's something wrong with you – it just means you're going through a normal phase that every single one of your friends is experiencing too.

The key is learning how to ride those emotional waves and cope with all the feelings in a healthy way. Maybe that means talking to a parent, teacher, or trusted friend about what you're going through. Or perhaps you'll find solace in activities like sports, music, or journaling – anything that lets you release some of that pent-up energy and emotion positively.

It's also important to be patient with yourself. Puberty is a process, and those mood swings won't last forever. With time and practice, you'll learn to better manage your emotions and find more balance and stability.

In the meantime, try not to beat yourself up too much over those occasional outbursts or emotional moments. We've all been there, fellas. It's just part of the incredible journey you're on, transforming from a kid into a young man with all the complexities and depth of emotion that come with it.

So, buckle up, take a deep breath, and get ready to ride those emotional waves like a pro surfer. Puberty might be a wild ride, but it's also an amazing, once-in-a-lifetime experience that's helping to shape you into the awesome person you're becoming.

Embrace the chaos, laugh at the mood swings, and know that you've got this – because you're stronger and more resilient than you could ever imagine.

Why Puberty Happens

You might be wondering why your body is going through this crazy thing called puberty in the first place. Well, believe it or not, it's all part of an amazing process that helps transform you from a kid into a full-grown adult!

Think of it this way: when you were little, your body was like a brand-new car fresh off the assembly line. It worked just fine for getting you around, but it didn't have all the bells and whistles that a souped-up, high-performance vehicle would have. Puberty is like an upgrade for your body, giving it all the new parts and features it needs to hit its stride.

This upgrade is kicked off by a tiny gland in your brain called the pituitary gland. Around the ages of 8-14 for guys, the pituitary starts pumping out special hormones that act like the mechanic working on your body's transformation. These hormones travel through your bloodstream, sending signals to different parts of your body to start changing and developing.

The hormones responsible for most of the puberty action in guys are called testosterone and growth hormone. Testosterone is the dude in charge of giving you deeper voices, bulking you up with more muscles, and triggering that facial and body hair growth. Growth hormone, on the other hand, is all about making you taller by helping your bones grow longer and stronger.

It's kind of like your body is getting a whole new engine, suspension system, and a fresh coat of paint all at once! Pretty awesome, right?

But puberty isn't just about the physical changes. Those same hormones also have an impact on your emotions, your interests, and even the way you think about things. It's like your brain is getting upgraded software to go along with your body's new hardware.

That's why you might find yourself feeling more independent, curious about romantic relationships, or drawn to new hobbies and interests during this time. Your mind is developing right along with your changing body, helping you grow into a unique individual with your personality and goals.

Of course, with all these incredible changes happening at once, it's only natural that puberty can feel a bit chaotic and overwhelming at times. But try to remember that it's all part of an amazing process that every single person goes through. You're not alone in this journey – your friends, classmates, and millions of other kids around the world are all transforming right alongside you.

So why does puberty happen? Because it's your body's way of leveling you up from a kid into a full-fledged adult, complete with all the awesome new abilities and experiences that come with it. It might be a wild ride, but it will ultimately shape you into the incredible person you're going to become.

Just think of it like a video game – you've made it to the next level, and while the challenges might be tougher, the rewards are even greater. So embrace the chaos, have fun with the changes, and get ready to unlock all the mind-blowing possibilities that come with being a teenager and young adult.

Chapter Two

Your Changing Body

Growing up is an incredible adventure, and your body is about to go through some mind-blowing changes! Puberty is like this amazing transformation where your body evolves from that of a kid into a full-fledged teenager. It's gonna get weird, it's gonna get wild, but trust me, it's all part of the awesome process of becoming a young man.

One of the biggest changes you'll notice is those growth spurts. Suddenly, you'll start shooting up like a beanstalk, leaving your old clothes in the dust. Your arms and legs will get longer, your hands and feet will seem massive, and you might even gain a few inches in height overnight! It's like your body is in a rush to catch up with the grown-up version of you.

And speaking of grown-ups, get ready for your voice to start changing too. You know how sometimes you'll be talking, and it'll crack or squeak most embarrassingly? That's because your vocal cords are getting thicker and longer, giving you that deep, manly tone you've always wanted. Sure, it might take some practice to control it at first, but soon enough, you'll be rocking that new voice like a pro.

Of course, with all these changes come some surprises too. Like body hair, for instance! One day, you'll look down and notice a few stray hairs popping up in places you've never had before – your armpits, your legs, and even your face! It might seem a little weird at first, but it's just your body's way of saying, "Hey, look at me, I'm becoming a man!"

And let's not forget about acne. Those pesky pimples and blemishes seem to pop up at the worst possible times, thanks to an increase in oil production caused by – you guessed it – those crazy puberty hormones. But don't worry, with a good skincare routine and a little patience, you'll get through this phase and come out on the other side with a clear, glowing complexion.

Speaking of hormones, they're also responsible for some of the emotional ups and downs you might be feeling during this time. One minute, you're on top of the world, and the next, you're moody, irritable, and ready to snap at the slightest thing. It's normal to experience mood swings and intense emotions as your brain chemistry shifts and adjusts to all the new changes happening in your body.

But here's the thing, guys: as wild and crazy as puberty might seem, it's all part of an incredible journey that every single person goes through. Your friends, your classmates, even your parents – they've all been through these same changes, and they made it to the other side just fine.

So, embrace the chaos! Laugh at the awkward moments, like when your voice cracks at the worst possible time or when you suddenly sprout a random hair in a weird place. Be patient with yourself as

you navigate these new emotions and physical transformations.

And most importantly, remember that you're not alone. We're all

in this together, and with a little guidance and a whole lot of

laughter, we'll make it through to the other side as awesome

young men.

Growing Pains: Dealing with Growth Spurts

One of the wildest parts of puberty is those crazy growth spurts!

It's like your body suddenly decides to hit the "grow" button, and

you start shooting up in height at an insane pace. Those long arms

and legs you've got now? Yeah, that's just your body's way of

saying, "Make way for the new, taller you!"

As awesome as it is to finally be one of the tallest kids in your class, these growth spurts can also come with some growing pains – literally. You might experience achy joints, sore muscles, and even the occasional stumble as you adjust to your new size. Don't worry, it's normal to feel a little uncoordinated and clumsy during this phase.

The key is to be patient with yourself and listen to your body. If you're feeling extra tired or achy, that's a sign you need to rest and let your body catch up with all the growing it's doing. Make sure you're staying active with plenty of stretching and light exercise to help alleviate some of those aches and pains.

And hey, if you ever feel a little self-conscious about your sudden height or those long limbs you're still getting used to, just remember – you're not alone! All your friends are going through the same thing, and before you know it, you'll all be towering over the adults in your life. So, embrace the growth spurt, stay positive, and know that this is just one more step in your incredible journey toward becoming a full-fledged teenager.

Voice Changes: Embracing Your New Sound

Your voice is about to go through a total transformation! You know that feeling when you're talking and suddenly your voice cracks or drops down an octave? That's because your vocal cords are getting longer and thicker, giving you that deep, manly tone you've always wanted.

At first, it might feel a bit strange and uncontrollable. One moment you'll sound like your normal self, and the next you'll be practically growling like a bear. But don't worry, that's all just part of the process. With time and practice, you'll learn to navigate those new low notes and own that resonating voice.

Embrace the change, my friends! Use it to your advantage when you want to sound extra cool or authoritative. And if your voice cracks mid-sentence? Just roll with it and laugh. Your friends are going through the same thing, so you might as well make a game out of seeing who can hit the widest range of notes.

Soon enough, you'll have that rich, mature voice that'll make you sound wise beyond your years. Just be patient, keep using those vocal cords, and get ready to leave your squeaky kid voice in the dust.

Hair Everywhere: Understanding Body Hair

At first, it might just be a few stray hairs here and there. But before you know it, you'll be dealing with a full-on mustache or beard situation. It's like your body is saying, "Hey, you're becoming a man now, so let's grow some manly hair to prove it!"

Don't be weirded out, though. Body hair is natural and just another sign that you're going through those incredible puberty changes. You should embrace it! That facial hair you're rocking? It's a badge of honor, showing the world that you're maturing into an awesome young dude.

Of course, with great facial hair comes great responsibility. You'll need to learn how to groom and maintain it properly. Invest in a good razor and some shaving cream, and don't be afraid to ask your dad or another trusted adult for tips on getting that clean, sharp look.

But most importantly, have fun with your new body hair! Give yourself a cool mustache or experiment with different beard styles. After all, it's just hair - if you don't like how it looks, you can always shave it off and start over. So rock that fuzz with confidence and pride, because it's all part of your incredible journey through puberty.

Acne and Skin Changes

You know those pesky pimples that seem to pop up at the most inconvenient times? Yeah, get ready for a lot more of those during puberty. As your body goes through all these intense changes, your skin is along for the ride too – and it's not always a smooth journey.

The main culprit behind acne is an increase in oil production triggered by those raging hormones. Your pores can get clogged more easily, leading to breakouts of whiteheads, blackheads, and those lovely pus-filled zits. Gross, I know, but it's all just part of the puberty package.

Don't stress too much about it, though! Acne is normal and happens to pretty much everyone at some point. Think of those pimples as temporary battle scars – annoying in the moment, but proof that you're becoming a young man.

The good news is, that with a solid skincare routine and a little patience, you can keep those breakouts under control. Wash your face regularly with a gentle, oil-free cleanser and use an over-the-counter spot treatment for any big zits that pop up. And hands off the popping! As tempting as it is, picking will only make things worse.

Your skin might also get a little greasier and sweatier thanks to those hard-working hormones. But again, it's no biggie – just make sure you're showering regularly and using a strong deodorant.

At the end of the day, try not to let acne get you down. You're going through a major life transformation, and a few temporary blemishes are a small price to pay for all the awesome changes happening in your body.

Body Odor and Hygiene

You're going to start noticing some funky new smells during puberty - and I'm not just talking about your friend's stinky feet! As your body matures and those hormones kick into high gear, you might find yourself dealing with a few odor issues of your own.

Get ready for things like sweaty armpits, stinky gym socks, and even a little extra musk "down there." It's all because of an increase in sweat and oil production that comes with puberty. Your body is working overtime, and unfortunately, some less-than-pleasant odors can tag along for the ride.

But don't stress - a little stink is normal! It just means your puberty journey is right on track. The key is staying on top of your hygiene game. Make sure you're showering regularly (like, every single day, dude) and using a strong deodorant and antiperspirant. Pick up some powder for those sweaty areas too.

Changing your clothes often, especially socks and underwear, is also a clutch for keeping funk at bay. And speaking of underwear - learn to love doing laundry, because those crusty skidmarks are not a good look for anyone.

It might seem like a lot of work, but keeping clean will make a world of difference in how you look, feel, and even smell as you navigate puberty. Plus, good hygiene is just part of growing into a

responsible young man. So step up your grooming game and be

proud of those new man-smells - just keep 'em under control.

Chapter Three

Navigating Emotions

Buckle up, because the emotional rollercoaster of puberty is about to take you on one wild ride! As your body goes through all these crazy physical changes, your brain decides to join the chaos by flooding you with a tsunami of new feelings and intense mood swings.

One minute, you're laughing hysterically with your friends over a silly joke. The next, you're fighting back angry tears because your mom asked you to take out the trash. Sound familiar? Welcome to the world of puberty emotions, where your feelings get amplified times a thousand!

It's like someone flipped an emotional switch, causing your brain to rapidly cycle through every possible mood and sentiment. You might feel invincible and on top of the world...only to crash into a pit of sadness or irritability moments later over something that normally wouldn't faze you. Talk about a mind-bending experience!

The reason for this emotional chaos? You guessed it - hormones! Those same chemical messengers telling your body to grow taller, sprout hair, and deepen your voice are also messing with the balance of brain chemicals that control your mood and emotions.

It's hormone overload, making you feel turbocharged with highs and lows you've never experienced before. And as unfair as it might seem, there's no way to control when these mood swings will strike or how intense they'll be.

You could be hanging with your friends one second, laughing it up and having an awesome time, when BAM - something as small as them teasing you about your new mustache triggers a blast of anger that makes you want to storm off in a rage. Uncool, right?

Or maybe you're playing your favorite video game, cruising through a tough level with focus and determination, when out of nowhere you're hit with this heavy wave of sadness or anxiety that makes it impossible to concentrate.

It's enough to make you feel like you're going crazy sometimes. But I promise, you're not! These mood swings are 100% normal and happen to everyone going through puberty. For real - even your calmest, most-together friend has dealt with bursts of intense emotions during this time.

The trick is learning to recognize when a mood swing is coming on so you can ride it out instead of letting it completely consume you. Maybe you need to take a breather and remove yourself from a situation for a little bit. Or perhaps talking it out with a friend or trusted adult will help relieve some of that pent-up angst.

Finding healthy outlets like exercise, art, music, or journaling can also be amazing ways to express those big emotions positively. As much as it might not feel like it sometimes, what you're experiencing is just a temporary phase.

With time, patience, and practice, you'll learn to better understand and manage those hormone-fueled mood swings. You'll become a master at recognizing your emotional triggers and knowing when you need to apply the brakes before you experience a total meltdown.

Most importantly, don't beat yourself up over the occasional outburst or mood swings. It happens to the best of us! Just dust yourself off, take a deep breath, and keep reminding yourself that you've got this. You're stronger and more resilient than you realize.

So buckle up and get ready for the emotional ride of your life! Sure, it might get bumpy and unpredictable at times. But by embracing the chaos and facing those mood swings head-on, you'll come out the other side as one well-adjusted, emotionally

mature dude.

Dealing with Stress and Anxiety

Feeling overwhelmed, anxious, or just plain stressed out lately?

Don't worry, you're not alone - puberty can seriously amp up

those not-so-fun emotions. As your body goes into transformation

mode, pumping out new hormones left and right, your brain gets

thrown for a loop too. Suddenly, things that never used to bother

you start feeling like a really big deal.

Maybe you get super anxious before presenting that class project,

even though public speaking used to be no sweat. Or perhaps you

lie awake at night, unable to quiet your racing thoughts about an

upcoming test or social situation. For some of us, anxiety and stress can even manifest as physical symptoms like headaches, stomachaches, or unexplained aches and pains.

The reality is, that these feelings are normal - and expected - when you're navigating the hormonal hurricane of puberty. Your brain is being flooded with new chemicals that can heighten your emotions and make you feel on edge more often. It's like your mind is a car stuck in the slow lane, trying to keep up with your body's speedy transformations.

But that doesn't mean you have to just white-knuckle it through the stress and worry. There are plenty of tips and tools you can use to keep anxiety at bay during this chapter. One of the best? Learning how to pause and practice some simple breathing exercises or meditation. Taking a few minutes to focus just on your inhales and exhales can work wonders for hitting the reset button on an overwhelmed mind.

Finding a hobby or creative outlet, like art, music, reading, or writing, is another awesome way to relieve pent-up stress. Anything that lets you get out of your head for a while and just zone out into an activity you enjoy can be a game-changer. Exercise is hugely helpful too - all those endorphins floating around have a way of naturally mellowing you out.

If anxiety or obsessive worrying starts disrupting your day-to-day, don't be afraid to open up about what you're feeling. Talking to a parent, teacher, counselor or other trusted adult lets you get it all out in the open and get some valuable perspective. Just articulating your churning thoughts and emotions out loud can bring so much relief.

There's also nothing wrong with practicing a little self-care when you're in one of those stressful funks. Maybe that looks like chilling out with a funny movie, listening to calming music, or just doing something relaxing that you enjoy. The key is recognizing your limits and knowing when to hit pause so you can re-center yourself.

Because at the end of the day, as intense as they might feel, these anxious thoughts and stressful situations are only temporary blips on your radar. With the right tools and mindset, you can power through the toughest moments puberty throws your way and come out stronger on the other side. Cut yourself some slack, be patient, and don't let stress steal your joy.

Expressing Your Feelings

Keeping all those big feelings bottled up inside during puberty? Yeah, that's a recipe for an emotional explosion just waiting to happen. The truth is, as uncomfortable as it might seem, learning how to express yourself healthily is crucial for navigating this rollercoaster ride.

I get it - opening up and being vulnerable doesn't exactly come naturally to most of us guys. We've been taught from an early age to keep a stiff upper lip, suck it up, and avoid showing any signs of weakness or sensitivity. But here's the thing: constantly burying your emotions is like shaking up a soda can and never opening it for release. Eventually, all that pressure is going to make you burst.

During puberty, you're experiencing a total mind-and-body overhaul, complete with crazy hormone surges that amplify every feeling times a thousand. Anger, sadness, anxiety, frustration - those tough emotions can hit with the force of a truck if you don't have a healthy outlet. Trying to just "tough it out" and ignore what's going on inside often leads to lashing out, withdrawing from friends and family, or developing unhealthy coping mechanisms down the road.

The alternative? Permitting yourself to feel your feelings, no matter how big, small, or irrational they might seem in the moment. Get comfortable sitting with uncomfortable emotions instead of running from them. Because as scary as it can be to confront the stuff you've been trying to avoid, the reality is that forming this deeper emotional awareness now will serve you for the rest of your life.

A great first step is simply setting aside some "you" time every day to do an emotional check-in. Whether you talk things out loud, write them down in a journal, or just sit and reflect, give yourself the space to get in touch with your inner world. Notice how you're feeling physically and mentally. Don't judge the emotions that come up or try to rationalize them away - just let them be.

From there, look for productive ways to work through and express those feelings. If you're angry or frustrated, go for a run or do some other physical activity to burn off steam. Feeling sad or anxious? Put on some chill music, call up a friend, or draw/paint your feelings out. You can even start a conversation with someone you trust about what's going on.

The key is finding the emotional outlets that work for you. Not everyone is comfortable diving deep into one-on-one convos or group therapy sessions. Maybe you'd rather write poetry, sing heartfelt lyrics, or take solace in nature. However you choose to express yourself, the act of letting those feelings out in a safe, healthy way is what matters most.

At the end of the day, recognizing and sitting with your emotions is what separates the guys who merely survive puberty from those who emerge as resilient, self-aware young men. It's a skill that will serve you well beyond these transformative years. So don't be afraid to get in touch with your feelings and let them out - your overall wellness depends on it. Just watch how much lighter and freer you'll feel.

Healthy Coping Mechanisms

Navigating all the ups and downs of puberty can feel like an emotional marathon some days. One minute, you're riding high on confidence and unstoppable energy. The next? You're hit with a tidal wave of anger, sadness, or crippling anxiety that knocks you off course. It's enough to make anyone want to hide under the covers and quit this whole "growing up" thing altogether.

But don't throw in the towel just yet! The key to surviving puberty's mood swings with your sanity intact is developing an arsenal of healthy coping tools to get you through the toughest moments. Think of them like superpowers you can activate anytime those big, overwhelming emotions strike.

One of the most powerful? Exercise. Yeah, I know working up a sweat might be the last thing on your mind when you're feeling down. But trust me, getting your body moving by shooting hoops, going for a jog, or even just dancing around like a lunatic can be crazy effective for battling stress, anger, and anxiety. Exercise causes your brain to release many mood-boosting chemicals, making you feel calmer and more centered in no time.

If getting physical isn't your vibe, try channeling your emotions through creative expression instead. Grab some art supplies and put those feelings into drawings or paintings. Write angsty poetry or lyrics to capture exactly what's going on inside you. Or shred on the guitar/drums/any instrument and just let loose! Pouring your heart into an artistic outlet gives your emotions somewhere safe and productive to go.

For the days when you're feeling especially wound up or scattered, disconnecting from technology with some mindfulness practices can be clutch. Spend a few minutes focused on taking deep, intentional breaths. Meditate or do some light yoga to get grounded in the present moment again. You'll be amazed at how much calmer and clear-headed you feel after just 10 minutes unplugged.

At the other end of the spectrum, venting to friends or family members you trust can provide much-needed release when you've got too much bottled up inside. Let it all out - the embarrassing moments that have you feeling insecure, the frustrations with parents/teachers you can't shake, the stress over schoolwork, or the social drama that's eating you alive. Sharing your burdens in a judgment-free space with people who care about you does wonders.

Of course, there will inevitably be days when none of the usual coping mechanisms seem to do the trick. That's when a little self-care and alone time can go a long way. Take a relaxing bath, read an engrossing book, listen to peaceful music, or do anything else that helps calm and recharge you. It's ok to need to retreat inward sometimes.

The main thing to remember is that however you choose to deal with, avoiding or numbing difficult emotions through unhealthy habits like zoning out in front of screens for hours, binge-eating junk, or lashing out at others will only make things worse in the long run. Riding the waves of puberty requires being proactive about processing every feeling that comes up.

So next time you're hit with a tidal wave of intense feels, activate one of your superpowers instead of crashing. Take a deep breath and trust that any storm is only temporary - with the right coping tools in your arsenal, you've got what it takes to power through toward clearer emotional skies ahead.

Chapter Four

Relationships and Social Changes

The teenage years are a wild time when it comes to friendships and social life. As you navigate puberty, you might notice some serious shifts happening in your relationships and how you feel about the people around you. It's all just part of the incredible growth and transition you're going through!

For a lot of guys, puberty marks the first time you start to feel interested in having a girlfriend or even just crushing hard on someone. Those newfound romantic feelings can seem confusing, exciting, and a little terrifying all at once. Will she like me back? What if I make a fool of myself? What does it even mean to "like-like" someone?!

Don't stress - having crushes and discovering your romantic side is normal during this phase. It just means you're becoming a young adult whose hormones are kicking into high gear. The key is learning how to handle those fluttery feelings in a respectful, mature way as you gain more experience.

Your perspectives on friendships might evolve during puberty too. People you used to be super tight with could start drifting as you find yourselves developing different interests or social circles. And that's okay! It's all part of figuring out who you are and surrounding yourself with people who genuinely vibe with the person you're becoming.

At the same time, you'll likely form some incredibly close bonds with new friends who just "get" everything you're going through - the mood swings, body changes, social pressures, and all. Don't be afraid to be vulnerable and open up with these friends. Having that core group who has your back no matter what during puberty will be invaluable.

Speaking of having people in your corner, don't be shy about leaning on family members, teachers, coaches, or other trusted adults when you need advice or just someone to listen. The teenage years can be socially tricky to navigate, but you don't have to go it alone.

Above all, remember that any friend or crush who makes you doubt yourself or treats you poorly is not worth stressing over. Prioritize the relationships that make you feel encouraged, accepted, and lifted for exactly who you are. With a little wisdom and self-confidence, you'll quickly learn how to cultivate a circle that brings out the best in you.

Sure, switching up your social life might mean making some tough decisions about who to spend time with and how to handle complicated situations. But don't let fear hold you back from putting yourself out there! This is your chance to start developing the communication skills and emotional intelligence that'll serve you for life.

Friends and Peer Pressure

Making good choices about who you hang out with and how you treat others becomes so important during the teenage years. As you go through puberty and start developing your own identity separate from your family, the friends you surround yourself with can have a huge impact - for better or worse.

On one hand, having a solid crew who shares your values and interests can be an incredible source of support, laughs, and confidence-boosting fun during this crazy transition. Friends who motivate you to chase your ambitions, try new things, and be the best version of yourself? Those are keepers for sure.

But on the flip side, falling in with the wrong crowd or giving in to unhealthy peer pressure can lead you down some paths you'll wish you never went near. Suddenly, you might find yourself doing things that go against your morals, just to fit in or impress others. Talking behind someone's back, experimenting with stuff you know is sketchy, or even bullying others - none of that is cool.

The reality is, peer pressure takes on a whole new dimension during puberty as you start craving autonomy and acceptance from your friend group above all else. You want so badly to belong and be seen as mature that it can cloud your judgment. But staying strong in your convictions and refusing to be a follower is what takes courage.

It all comes down to choosing your circle wisely and believing enough in yourself to walk away from any situation that makes you uncomfortable or disrespects who you are. Build a rock-solid group of friends who encourage you to dream big, work hard, and be nothing but authentically YOU - flaws, strengths, and all.

Those are the day ones who will always have your back, whether you're celebrating victories or going through struggles. They'll call you out when you're wrong but never pressure you into compromising your values just to look cool. More importantly, they'll inspire you to be that same loyal, confident, and principled friend in return.

Making smart social choices now about who you let influence you sets the stage for a lifetime of healthy relationships and a sense of self-worth. So look for friends who bring out the absolute best in you and have no problem walking away from anything negative. Navigating peer pressure like a pro? That's true maturity.

Dealing with Bullying

Bullying is one of the most difficult and painful things you can experience as a kid. Whether it's being teased, excluded, physically hurt, or targeted online, dealing with a bully can make you feel scared, alone, and utterly powerless. But here's the truth - you don't have to suffer in silence. There are ways to stand up to bullies and take back control.

The first step? Do not engage or retaliate with the bully directly. As tempting as it might be to fight fire with fire, that's only going to escalate the situation and potentially put you in harm's way. Bullies tend to feed off getting a rise out of their targets. Starve them of that reaction, and their power starts to diminish.

Instead, your best move is to create distance and remove yourself from the bully's vicinity as quickly as possible. Walk away confidently, don't make eye contact, and go somewhere you feel safe - whether that's around friends, a teacher, or another trustworthy adult. Bullies want to shake your self-esteem, so staying calm and unbothered shows you won't be an easy target.

From there, it's crucial that you speak up and tell someone about what's been happening. Parents, teachers, counselors, coaches - anyone you feel comfortable confiding in can help put a stop to the bullying behavior. Document everything with dates, times, locations, witnesses, and screenshots if it's happening online. The more evidence you can provide, the better.

Don't ever feel embarrassed about asking for help or like you have to go it alone. Bullying is never the victim's fault! Speaking out protects not just you, but any other kids who might be targets too. Schools and communities have rules and resources to deal with bullying effectively when they're made aware.

In the meantime, build up your crew of real friends who have your back and make you feel valued for who you are. Surround yourself with positive people and do more of what fulfills you. Bullies prey on insecurity, so boosting your self-worth and confidence is your biggest shield against their harsh words and actions.

You've got this! By refusing to suffer in silence, enforcing boundaries, and focusing on your passions rather than bullies' negativity, you can overcome them. Their behavior is a reflection of their struggles - don't let it dim your spirit. Stay strong in your truth, and their power over you will fizzle out before long. You're a trooper already for getting this far.

Understanding Romantic Feelings

Have random crushes and catching feelings for someone special? Welcome to the rollercoaster ride of the first romantic stirrings! As you enter puberty, get ready for a whirlwind of new thoughts and emotions around dating, relationships, and just general heart-fluttering over that cute person in your class.

It might seem bizarre and confusing at first. One minute, you're minding your own business. The next, you can't stop obsessing over how adorable their smile is or replaying tiny interactions with them over and over in your mind. Suddenly, handholding or sharing snacks takes on this huge, momentous meaning.

What you're experiencing is normal! As your brain gets a surge of new hormones, it's kickstarting your ability to develop deeper romantic interests and attractions beyond just platonic friendships.

Those giddy, flustered feelings are all part of the exciting rush of curiosity about dating and intimacy.

Of course, having a crush can also come with some embarrassing awkwardness and uncertainty. Will they like me back? What if I say or do something weird around them? How do I even go about asking them out?? Take a deep breath - you're not alone in getting flustered over this stuff.

The key is to just roll with those bashful moments when you can't seem to string two words together around your crush object. Laugh it off, remind yourself they're just a person too, and move forward being the friendly, authentic version of you that initially drew their interest. Confidence is super attractive, even if it's faked a little at first!

As intimidating as it might seem, don't be afraid to explore acting on those feelings in little ways too. Complimenting the person, asking them to hang out, or even sharing that you have a crush can feel scary but also incredibly liberating. You'll quickly learn there's nothing to fear in getting real with yourself and putting a little courage behind your heart's desires.

Most importantly, manage expectations if the feelings don't seem to be reciprocated - not every crush becomes a magical relationship. But don't let that discourage you! Take it as a growth opportunity to build resilience and keep putting yourself out there, even through rejection or heartbreak. The more you explore what it means to have romantic feelings, the closer you'll get to one day experiencing an amazing connection. Growing up is an adventure.

Communication Skills

Mastering the art of communication is one of the most valuable skills you can develop as you navigate the ups and downs of puberty and relationships. Sure, it might seem way easier to just grunt, shrug, or stare at your phone whenever someone tries to start a conversation. But learning how to express yourself through spoken and body language? That's a total game-changer.

Think about it - strong communication abilities help you articulate your thoughts and feelings in a way that deepens connections with friends, family, teachers, and romantic interests. You're able to get your point across clearly, while also making others feel heard and understood. Suddenly, complex emotions that once felt impossible to put into words start making more sense.

Engaging in face-to-face dialogue, maintaining eye contact, and using "I" statements to own your perspectives - these are all keys to becoming an effective communicator. It allows you to advocate for yourself, set boundaries, and avoid misunderstandings that can lead to conflicts down the line. Mastering confident body language and vocal tones conveys self-assurance too.

That's not to say you have to be a constant chatterbox! Listening intently and asking follow-up questions is just as crucial. Making others feel heard and valued when they're speaking, rather than planning your rebuttal or staring into space, creates a sincere two-way flow of dialogue. You'd be surprised how many friendships and relationships get stronger just through this simple act of being present.

Little habits like minimizing filler words ("um," "like," "you know"), putting down your phone when someone is talking, and maintaining an open posture all elevate your communication game. It shows you're truly invested in the conversation and respect whoever is speaking. These are talents that'll serve you for years.

Of course, becoming a stellar communicator takes practice. You're not going to nail it overnight, and that's perfectly OK! Have patience with yourself as you learn to make more eye contact or speak more slowly and clearly. If anxiety makes you freeze up sometimes, breathe through it. The more you flex those skills, the more naturally self-expression will start to feel.

At the end of the day, developing intelligence in how you relate to others, whether through an important conversation or just casual small talk, gives you invaluable confidence. You're able to cut through awkwardness, assert yourself, and start building the types of deep connections you crave as you grow up. It's one of the most significant superpowers you can acquire.

Chapter Five

Sexuality and Reproductive Health

As you go through puberty, you're going to start noticing some serious changes happening in your body related to sexuality and reproduction. Things like unexpected erections, wet dreams, and even self-exploration down there are normal at this stage. It's just your body's way of maturing and preparing for the years ahead.

While it can seem confusing or even embarrassing at first, try not to stress too much about these developments. They happen to literally every single guy as you transition into adolescence. The key is learning what's going on so you can understand and be in control of your changing body.

Those random erections, for example, are caused by spikes in male hormones like testosterone. It's a natural physical response, not something you can fully control yet. Wet dreams, where you ejaculate during sleep, are also your body's way of getting rid of older sperm. Not the most glamorous side of puberty, but it happens!

The main thing to know is that any questions, confusion, or concerns you have about these matters are 100% valid. Don't ever feel embarrassed about opening up to a parent, doctor, counselor, or other trusted adult for guidance. They can provide the facts while offering reassurance that you're developing perfectly normally.

Sexuality and all its complexities can seem daunting right now. But this period is just the start of an incredible journey getting to know yourself, your values, and how to approach relationships and intimacy in a safe, consensual way as you get older. Having a solid foundation of knowledge will allow you to make smart choices for your reproductive health.

So don't shy away from this topic! Puberty is when you begin learning to feel comfortable and empowered in your skin. Admitting you have questions and being proactive about your sexual well-being is part of growing into the awesome young man you're becoming.

Understanding Your Body

Let me try this again in a more conversational tone:

Puberty is a wild ride, isn't it fellas? Your body is going through some major changes, and it can feel pretty crazy at times. But don't sweat it - I'm here to walk you through it all.

As a mom who's seen my son go through puberty, I know exactly what you're dealing with. One of the biggest things is that growth spurt. Boom - suddenly your arms and legs feel like they belong to a giant! Your body is hitting a major growth spurt, stretching you out overnight. Those growing pains are no joke, but they'll calm down once your body adjusts to its new size.

Then there's your voice. Remember when you used to sound like a little chipmunk? Well, get ready for it to start cracking and deepening into a grown man's voice. It's like your vocal cords are going through puberty too! One morning you'll wake up sounding different. Weird, but also kind of cool, right?

You might also notice hair popping up in new places - your armpits, legs, maybe even your face. Don't freak out - it just means you're becoming a young dude. We'll get you started on shaving before too long.

Of course, puberty also brings some other fun stuff, like acne. Those zits are annoying, I know, but we can help keep your skin looking fresh with some good face-washing habits. No popping though, you'll just make it worse!

With all the changes, you might start smelling a bit...ripe. That's your body's sweat and oils kicking into overdrive as you grow up. Normal, but a good reminder to hop in the shower regularly and use deodorant.

I know it's a lot, but you've got this! Puberty happens to every guy. If you ever feel overwhelmed or have questions, come talk to me.

Changes in Sexual Development

During puberty, you're going to notice some big changes happening "down there" as you start developing into a young man. I know it can feel awkward or even a little scary, but these changes are normal and natural.

As you go through puberty, your testicles will get bigger and start producing sperm cells and testosterone. Testosterone is the hormone that gives you a deeper voice, body hair, and other manly traits. Your penis will also grow longer and wider during this time.

You might wake up with your first "wet dream" which is when semen (that liquid containing sperm) comes out while you're sleeping. It's normal and just your body's way of getting rid of older sperm. It can be a little messy, but nothing to be embarrassed about.

As your body matures, you'll likely start getting erections more often, even when you're not thinking sexual thoughts. This happens because increased testosterone makes it easier to get erections from just about anything. They usually go away quickly, but if not, think about something else or do an activity until it passes.

You might also notice a collection of smegma under your foreskin if you're uncircumcised. This is just dead skin cells and oils - be sure to gently pull back your foreskin and clean it daily in the shower. Using mild soap and water prevents infections or unpleasant odors.

I know this stuff can seem embarrassing to talk about, but it's so important you understand what's happening. Your body is preparing for the ability to reproduce one day way down the road. For now, focus on taking care of yourself through this transition. If any questions come up, I'm here to provide the facts.

Consent and Boundaries

Consent and boundaries. As you get older and start having crushes or romantic feelings, it's crucial to understand how to respect boundaries, both your own and others.

Consent means freely giving permission or agreeing to something. When it comes to any kind of physical interaction like hugging, kissing, or more, you need to make sure the other person consents and is comfortable too. It has to be an enthusiastic "Yes!" from both people. Anything less than that is not true consent.

No one should ever pressure, trick, or force you into any activity you don't want to do. Your body is yours, and you get to set the boundaries for what you're okay with. Don't let anyone make you feel guilty or obligated. "No means no" - always respect if someone isn't into what's happening.

At the same time, you need to pay close attention to the other person's body language and boundaries too. If they seem uncomfortable, uncomfortable or are giving you a weird vibe, stop what you're doing. Check in and make sure they're good to keep going. The idea is to make sure you both feel safe, respected, and happy with what's happening.

It's also important to remember that consent has to happen every single time, even with the same person. Just because someone said yes before doesn't mean they automatically want to do that activity again. You have to get their okay first.

I know this consent stuff might seem overboard for stuff like hand-holding or hugs. But the sooner you start practicing checking in and being mindful of boundaries, the better. These skills will be so valuable as you get older.

If you ever feel pressured, threatened, or taken advantage of - even by a friend - tell a trusted adult right away. And if you're ever unsure about a situation, don't hesitate to ask me or another grown-up you trust. We want to equip you with the knowledge to make good choices and be respectful of yourself and others. Your bodily autonomy matters.

Safe Sex and Protection

While sex itself may still seem a long way off, we must talk about safe sex and protection now so you have a solid understanding before those situations potentially come up down the road.

Even though you're still young, bodies can physically be capable of sexual activity during and after puberty. That's why we need to cover things like preventing sexually transmitted infections (STIs) and unexpected pregnancies from a factual, open perspective.

When two people decide they are ready for sexual intimacy, there are few effective ways to stay safe. Using condoms every single time is crucial - they protect against STIs like chlamydia and HIV which can have really serious health consequences. Putting on a condom properly is something we can practice together using examples.

For pregnancy prevention, your best route is abstinence - simply not having sex. But if you do decide to be sexually active someday, condoms combined with another contraceptive method like the pill give you maximum protection against both STIs and unwanted pregnancy.

The key thing to remember is that safe sex requires planning, communication, and responsibility from both partners. It's not at all a sure thing that protection will be used properly in the heat of the moment unless you make it a serious priority ahead of time. Consequences like infections or pregnancies at a young age can derail your life in major ways.

I know this is very grown-up stuff, but I want to prepare you with facts while your brain is developed enough to digest this information. I hope that by addressing boundaries, safe practices, and the gravity of sexual intimacy now, you'll have a strong foundation of knowledge to make smart choices for yourself when the time comes.

Remember, you can always come to me with any other questions on this topic. There's no need to feel awkward or afraid to ask the difficult things. I'm your mom and my role is to equip you to navigate relationships and sex responsibly. We're in this together.

Chapter Six

Taking Care of Yourself

It's so important to take care of yourself - both physically and mentally. Puberty can feel like an emotional rollercoaster, but making healthy choices will help you feel your best.

First up, let's talk about food and exercise. Your body needs good fuel from nutritious meals and snacks to keep growing properly. But you also need to stay active through sports, gym class, or just playing outside with friends. Finding that balance of eating well and moving your body is key.

Sleep is another crucial piece of the self-care puzzle. I know you may feel invincible, but your mind and body recharge best when you get 8-10 hours each night. Not getting quality zzz's can mess with your mood, energy levels, and ability to learn.

Don't forget to also make time to just chill and decompress. Puberty's changes can feel overwhelming, so do activities that calm your mind like reading, listening to music, or just hanging out sans screens. If you're feeling super stressed, talk to me or another trusted adult about it.

At the end of the day, puberty is a marathon, not a sprint. Be kind to yourself as you adjust to your new, changing body. This won't last forever, but taking care of your total well-being now will make the journey so much smoother.

Healthy Eating and Exercise

When it comes to eating well during puberty, it's all about fueling your body with the right stuff to support your growing and changing needs. You're going through a major growth spurt, so getting enough nutrients is key.

Protein is hugely important for building strong muscles and bones as you sprout up. Lean meats like chicken or turkey, eggs, beans, nuts, and dairy products like milk and yogurt are all excellent protein sources. Don't be afraid to load up on them! Your body craves that muscle-building fuel.

You also need plenty of vitamins and minerals from fruits and veggies to keep your body systems running smoothly. I know produce can seem lame, but there are lots of tasty ways to eat it - fresh, cooked, blended into smoothies, you name it. Having a colorful variety gives you different vitamins.

And don't forget about those whole grains! Things like oats, brown rice, and whole wheat bread/pasta provide long-lasting energy from fiber and complex carbs. They'll help power you through active days way better than sugary snacks that make you crash.

Speaking of activity, exercise is so important when you're going through puberty. Your body is going through a major overhaul and moving helps manage strength, flexibility, endurance, and weight as you grow.

Team sports are an amazing way to stay fit while learning teamwork and making new friends. Whether it's soccer, basketball, swimming, or something else, find an activity you genuinely enjoy and stick with it.

If team sports aren't your thing, no worries! Going for daily walks or bike rides, shooting hoops, or following along with workout videos all count too. The key is finding consistency with whatever movement you choose. Even just 60 minutes of heart-pumping activity each day gives you a ton of benefits.

It's also great to mix in some strength training as you get older by using resistance bands or light weights. This builds muscle mass and bone density during your critical growth years. Just be sure to use proper form to avoid injuries.

I know eating well and exercising regularly can feel like a drag sometimes. But taking care of your body's needs now sets you up for a lifetime of feeling energized, strong, and confident in your changing body. Don't be afraid to get creative in the kitchen and with your workouts either - it'll make the whole process feel way more fun.

Getting Enough Sleep

Sleep is one of the most important things for your growing body during puberty, but I know it can be seriously tough to get enough zzz's with everything going on. Between hormones, homework, and just feeling wired, sufficient sleep often gets pushed aside. But staying well-rested is crucial for your mental health, growth, and overall functioning.

Experts recommend 8-10 hours per night for kids your age. I know that seems like an eternity when you're socially active and have a million things you'd rather be doing. But cutting corners on sleep can leave you feeling foggy, sluggish, moody, and straight-up awful the next day. Not worth it!

Creating a relaxing pre-bed routine can make it much easier to wind down at night. Things like taking a warm shower/bath, reading fiction for fun, listening to chill music, or doing simple stretches all signal to your body that it's hibernation time. Just avoid heavy exercise or stimulating activities right before bed.

If racing thoughts are keeping you awake, try writing in a journal to get worries off your mind. Or do some deep breathing exercises to calm your nervous system. Sometimes dimming lights and playing ambient sound can help too. Do whatever rituals allow your mind and body to truly relax into restorative sleep.

Getting adequate rest is one of the kindest things you can do for yourself through these transformative puberty years. Your mind and body will thank you.

Self-Care and Mental Health

Being a tween is stressful enough with all the friend drama, school pressures, and figuring out who you are. Add raging hormones and awkward physical shifts into the mix and your brain can go into straight-up chaos mode. One minute you're happy, the next you're angry or sad for no apparent reason. It's enough to make anyone's head spin!

The key is finding healthy ways to process and cope with these intense thoughts and feelings as they arise. Things like journaling, talking to a parent or counselor, or practicing mindfulness through deep breathing or meditation can be game-changers. Getting those anxious thoughts or big emotions out, instead of bottling them up, provides massive relief.

Making time for activities that calm and recharge your mind is also a must. Maybe it's listening to chill music, reading for fun, playing a sport you love, or just hanging with friends who make you laugh. Having positive outlets gives your brain a break from the puberty pressure cooker.

It's also so important to be kind and patient with yourself. Your changing brain is quite literally under construction, so obsessing over every missed social cue or imperfection is counterproductive. Cut yourself some slack and celebrate small wins each day, even if it's just taking a shower or getting dressed. You're doing hard work!

Please know you don't have to tough it out alone. If negative thought patterns, irritability, or persistent sadness linger for more than a couple of weeks, tell me or another trusted adult. There's no shame in asking for help - everyone needs professional support sometimes, especially during the turbulence of puberty. Working with a counselor provides guidance and proven strategies.

At the end of the day, looking after your mental wellbeing needs to be a top priority as you navigate this wild phase of life. Have compassion for yourself, lean on your support squad, and don't be afraid to speak up if you need more help. I'm always here with a listening ear and endless empathy. We'll get through these years together, one deep breath at a time.

Setting Goals and Building Confidence

I'll let you in on a secret - pretty much every guy feels awkward and unsure during puberty. You're not alone in dealing with things like voice cracks, sprouting hair, acne, and general self-consciousness about your changing appearance. What separates the confident guys from the insecure ones is their mindset.

Don't get me wrong, positive thinking alone won't magically solve everything. But making an intentional effort to focus on your strengths, channeling energy into productive goals, and being kinder to yourself in self-talk makes a huge difference.

Start by making a list of what you're naturally good at - maybe it's art, music, math, athletics, creative writing, or just being a loyal friend. Chances are you downplay your talents more than you realize. Seeing them written out provides an instant confidence boost by highlighting your unique abilities.

From there, set some achievable goals to further develop those strengths and interests over the next few months or years. Having a specific skill to work toward, like getting better at coding, cooking vegetarian meals, or training for a 5K gives you a healthy channel for your ambition and self-improvement.

Hitting those incremental milestones you set, no matter how small provides a constant source of pride and motivation to keep leveling up. You'll be amazed at how much progress compounds over time when you apply consistent effort.

It's equally important to celebrate non-skill wins too. Maybe your goal is showing more kindness to your siblings, using better study habits, or keeping your temper in check more often. Recognizing inner growth and maturity is an underrated confidence booster.

Of course, there will be setbacks and awkward moments along the way - that's puberty for you. The key is going easier on yourself and changing that overly critical inner monologue. Would you talk to a friend the way you insult yourself sometimes? Probably not, so have some empathy!

Building true confidence is an endless journey of working on your skills, mental game, and self-perception. But taking those first steps now to set goals, appreciate your unique talents, and be kinder to yourself provides lifelong benefits. I'm here to support you every step of the way as you blossom into your most assured,

authentic self. You've got this.

Chapter Seven

Talking with Adults

Talking to adults about the changes you're going through can feel awkward and uncomfortable. Believe me, I remember how mortifying it was at your age to discuss anything even remotely related to puberty, relationships, or the other grown-up topics in this book. But having open, honest conversations is so important.

The reality is, that the adults in your life - whether that's me, your dad, relatives, teachers, coaches, or counselors - want to create a safe space for you to get answers and guidance. We've been through puberty ourselves and know how confusing and overwhelming this transition can be. Our role is to take the embarrassment out of it and provide you with the facts, advice, and reassurance you need.

Don't ever hesitate to ask us questions, no matter how awkward or silly you think they may sound. There's no such thing as a dumb question when you're navigating something as complex as puberty. We'd much rather you get information from trusted sources than rumors or misinformation online or from friends.

Our door is always open to discuss sensitive topics without judgment. Whether it's about friend drama, bodily changes, sexuality, mental health issues, or self-confidence - we can handle it. The lines of communication need to go both ways for us to understand what you're experiencing.

Think of the adults in your life as members of your personal puberty support team. We're here to listen, support you, and provide a safe space to become the amazing young man you're becoming.

Communicating with Parents or Guardians

I want to avoid those cringe-worthy conversations at all costs! But as much as it might make you want to run for the hills, having open and honest chats with the adults in your life is so important during this transition.

Your parents or guardians were once clueless kids going through puberty too. They've walked in your shoes and want to be a supportive resource as your body and emotions do this wild transformation. Sure, it may seem like they have no idea what you're going through, but I promise they have way more wisdom and perspective to share than you think.

The key is learning how to communicate effectively so you both feel comfortable. If certain subjects, like talking about bodily changes or sexuality, make you want to spontaneously combust from embarrassment, try writing your questions down first. Having a physical note can make it easier to address rather than staring your parents in the eye.

You can also look for natural conversation starters when watching TV shows or movies that bring up relevant puberty topics. Using scenes as a way to bring up your curiosities or experiences can make the chat feel more casual.

And please, don't stress about finding the perfect wording to ask something. Your parents care way more that you're being open with them than whether you use all the medical terminology correctly. They'd much rather you ask them directly about sensitive subjects than get misinformation elsewhere.

It's also so important to be honest if you're struggling with things like stress, anxiety, body image issues, or friend drama. As awkward as it is, your parents can't help guide you through these rough patches if you keep your feelings bottled up inside. Think of how worried you'd be if they were going through a hard time alone.

I know it can be really hard to see your parents as anything other than figures of authority sometimes. But they love you unconditionally and genuinely want to support you however they can during this crazy transition. Having their wisdom, empathy, and life experience in your corner is such a valuable gift - even if you have to push past the occasional eye-roll or cringe-fest to get there.

Trusted Adults, You Can Talk To

Navigating puberty can feel like being stuck in a crazy maze, with new twists and turns popping up daily. That's why having a circle of trusted adults to talk to, besides your parents, is so valuable during this time. They provide additional support, perspective, and guidance as you try to make sense of your changing body, emotions, and experiences.

Teachers and school counselors are a great place to start when you need an understanding adult ear. They have training to address the issues young guys face with sensitivity and without judgment. Don't be afraid to approach them about friend issues, academic stress, bodily changes, or anything else on your mind. Their role is to create a safe space for you to open up.

Coaches, youth group leaders, relatives, and family friends can also be wonderful sources of wisdom about maturity and manhood. Since they're a degree removed from your day-to-day life, you may feel more comfortable confiding in them about certain topics than your parents at times. Their insights from personal experience are priceless.

The key is identifying a few grown-ups you fully trust and feel at ease around. They should be people you know will guard your privacy and provide honest, caring advice tailored just for you - not what they think you want to hear. You need to feel completely comfortable being vulnerable and asking them personal questions.

Once you've picked your puberty mentors, don't be afraid to use them! Check-in regularly to get their take on whatever's going on, from the hilariously awkward to the deadly serious. An impartial sounding board is invaluable for clearly seeing situations and choices, instead of getting trapped in your head.

What you discuss stays confidential unless they think you could be in danger. So be upfront about what's happening in your world, even the embarrassing stuff. These are your hand-picked experts on this crazy phase of life - let them be your guides!

At the end of the day, the puberty journey is a lot easier when you've got a small team of caring adults you can turn to for support and straight answers, no matter how cringey the topic.

Asking Questions and Seeking Help

Asking questions and seeking help about the wild world of puberty can feel super awkward and uncomfortable. Believe me, I get it - there's nothing worse than having to discuss things like bodily changes, relationships, or embarrassing personal issues with adults when you're at this age.

But as bizarre and cringeworthy as it may seem, being open to asking trusted adults for guidance and information is so important during this transition. Puberty brings up a ton of new situations and experiences that you've never had to navigate before. Having a support system to turn to prevents you from stumbling through it alone and potentially making decisions you regret.

The reality is, that the adults in your life desperately want you to ask them anything on your mind, no matter how awkward or silly you think it may be. Your parents, relatives, teachers, counselors, and other mentors have been through puberty themselves. They know first-hand how confusing and overwhelming this stage of life feels. Their role is to make you comfortable enough to openly discuss personal issues without shame or judgment.

So don't ever self-censor or hold back from raising your hand for help, whether it's a burning question about bodily changes, sexuality, mental health, relationships, or just general growing pains. There's no such thing as a stupid query - any topic related to your personal growth and well-being is 100% valid. The only silly questions are the ones you keep bottled up inside.

The adults around you would much rather you get information from them as first-hand, trustworthy resources than rumors from peers or sketchy online sources. Their doors are always open to have open, honest conversations to ensure you get facts, not misinformation.

At the end of the day, your personal puberty support team is here to provide guidance, reassurance, and a safe space to work through any issues on your mind. Don't be afraid to use them! Asking questions and advocating for the help you need is a sign of courage and maturity. We're in this together to navigate the choppy waters of adolescence. You've got this.

Conclusion

We've covered a lot of ground talking about the wild ride of puberty. From the awkward physical and emotional changes to navigating relationships and sexual health to taking care of yourselves mentally and physically - I've tried to prepare you guys for pretty much anything this transition could throw your way.

But if there's one big takeaway I want you to internalize, it's this: You are not alone in this experience. I can't emphasize that enough. Every single person - including me, my friends, athletes, celebrities, you name it - has been through the weirdness and insecurity of puberty. We've all dealt with cracking voices, smelly pits, wildly fluctuating moods, and endless awkwardness. It's the great glamorous equalizer!

So whenever you're feeling like a freakish outsider trapped in your changing body, remember that literally every other guy your age is going through some variation of the same thing. You've got an instant brotherhood of puberty partners surrounding you, even if you can't see it. We're all in this together, learning how to adapt to our new voices, bigger bodies, funny hair patterns, and surging thoughts/emotions daily.

The key is embracing it all with confidence, patience, and a good sense of humor. Yeah, puberty is weird and messy - but it's also an awesome experience getting to develop into a young man. This is the chrysalis stage where you recreate your identity, strengths, and interests before emerging as your true self. That's pretty freakin' amazing if you ask me!

So don't resist the changes - lean into them. Let your awkwardness shine and roll with each new development, because that's just part of the process. If you can get comfortable inhabiting your vulnerabilities now, it'll serve you forever down the line. Authenticity, self-acceptance, and inner confidence for the win!

Of course, that's way easier said than done some days. I remember my son frequently feeling like a stranger in his skin and mind during puberty. But having a strong system of supportive adults around him made all the difference. We emphasized that the hardships he was facing were universally shared, temporary, and serving an important growth purpose. The dust eventually settles - you just have to make it through!

Once you emerge from the puberty storm, there's an exciting new chapter of youth ahead. You'll start truly finding your voice and self-confidence. Relationships, independence, and big life decisions like college or career paths will come into focus. It's an amazing phase of exploring your identity and passions with new maturity.

But that transition is still a ways off. For now, the journey is the destination, fellas. Soak up all the lessons and personal growth opportunities puberty is throwing your way. Get comfortable being uncomfortable, because overcoming awkwardness builds resilience. Lean on your system of supportive adults for wisdom and guidance along the way.

More than anything, just vow to give yourself endless grace. Puberty is one of life's most seismic transitions - you're becoming an entirely new person in a very short period. That's bound to create confusion and serious growing pains, both physical and emotional. But you've got this. Pretty soon, you'll be men out in the world, armed with all the skills and self-knowledge this profound metamorphosis provided. The present is temporary, but the future is brilliantly yours! Embrace every single step.

Made in the USA
Las Vegas, NV
18 May 2024

90089994R00066